Emmanuelle Ayrton

D0433057

Silence!
Singers at Work

A singer's sketchbook

PETERS EDITION LTD
A member of the EDITION PETERS GROUP
LEIPZIG · LONDON · NEW YORK

Published by
Peters Edition Limited
2–6 Baches Street
London
N1 6DN
www.editionpeters.com

First published 2014
© Copyright 2014 by Emmanuelle Ayrton
ISBN 1-84367-051-3
A catalogue record for this book is available from the British Library

To those who dare, and give...

*L*aughter, heartache, effervescence, sacrifice, passion, betrayal, lust, joy, tears, euphoria, scrutiny, desire: welcome to the explosive world of the classically trained singer!

We are those sometimes skittish, often dramatically flamboyant characters who carry our fragile, invisible instrument around with us for every single second of the day and night, while an ever present, finicky spotlight of criticism constantly hovers over us, ready to pounce on our every misstep while we tread cautiously over the most narrow, flimsy tightrope of vocal technique in order to move the hungry listener to tears, or transport them into unbridled ecstasy.

We travel the world in solitude, passing hours in the lonely studio to perfect our "Ah" vowel, and to conquer the most onerous musical phrases requiring the breath control of Olympic athletes. We sweat hours in the gym in order to convincingly portray a 14-year-old pre-pubescent boy chasing anything in a skirt, or an 18-year-old girl dying of consumption who must sing a marathon of treacherous vocalism before finally ceding to death's call 45 minutes later. We engage in constant, painful self-reflection in order to moult the layers of self-criticism and doubt that prevent us from the freedom of expression we need in order to make the potent emotions soar through our vocal cords.

We juggle a multitude of languages, cross five centuries of musical styles, project without amplification over a symphony of upwards of 100 instruments, lay ourselves utterly bare in front of thousands of critical spectators ~ and we do it because we LOVE it, we NEED it, and we can't possibly imagine doing anything else.

We are Classical Singers, and this is our WORLD!

Joyce DiDonato

The dog barks,
the cat meows,
the owl hoots,
the frog croaks,
the mouse squeaks,
the horse neighs,
the donkey brays,
the cow moos,
the hippopotamus bellows,
the cockerel crows,
the rabbit drums,
the pig snorts,
the ape gibbers,
the sheep bleats,
the wolf howls,
the dove coos,
the blackbird whistles,
the blue-tit warbles,
the warbler babbles,
the camel grunts,
the elephant trumpets,
the lion roars,
the turkey gobbles,
the cicada chirps,
the swallow twitters,
the fly buzzes,
the wasp hums,
the hyena laughs,
the bat screeches,
the penguin calls,
the linnet chuckles,

and man, sometimes, sings...

13 minutes to go...

too hot

too cold

Spring

Summer

Autumn

Winter

my finger slipped

everyone's fault but mine

memorization

insomnia

nightmare no. 1: "curtain in two minutes"

nightmare no. 2

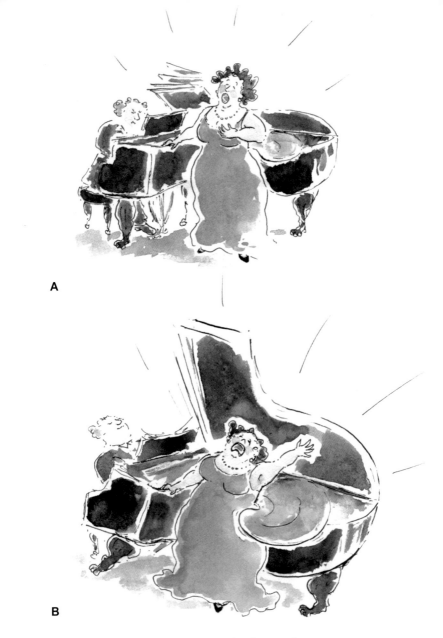

A

B

nightmare no. 3: broken cadence

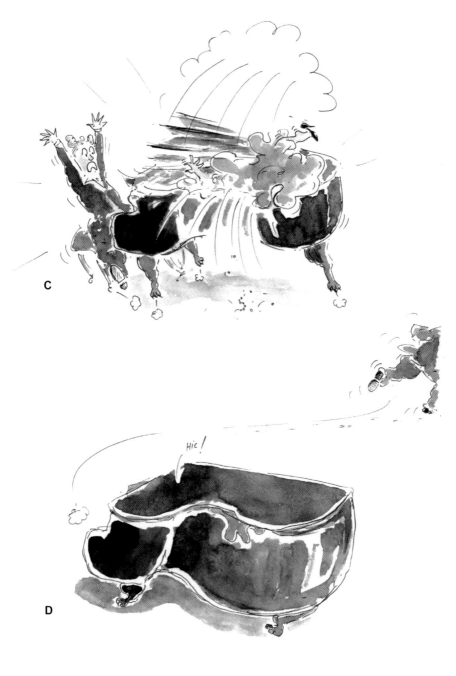

C

D

Hic!

21

nightmare audition (for real)

" We're looking for a singer with experience in the role,
but something of a blank slate. We have a concept, you see.
You'll need to be able to dance en pointe in a negligee,
and lose 10 pounds for the camera.
We know the room is carpeted,
but if you could project as if you were on stage..."

backstage

the crucial moment

2,300 Hz

Springtime

ACCESSORIES

A 440 Hz **A 4IS Hz**

training bra

church survival gear

I shriek therefore I am

breathing space

novice

Soloists:

a soloist in spite of himself

If you missed it the first time, have a closer look! Or make an appointment with your optician...

involuntary solo

The Soloist

points of view

conductor's despair

STAGE
ENTRANCE

DIVA EXIT

TENOR AHEAD
GIVE
WAY

MEZZOS

ENGAGE
LOWER GEAR

80

OPERATIC BARITONE
HIGH WINDS

BASSO PROFONDO

CAUTION
DRAMATIC SOPRANO IN ACTION
DOUBLE HEARING
PROTECTION
REQUIRED
IN THIS AREA

PITCH!

 Learner

THE TROUBLE WITH BEING A SINGER

acute laryngitis

runny nose

concert cancelled

seasonal paranoia

RECITAL CLOTHES

MAN

choice A   or   B

a day in the life of a Diva (1)

a day in the life of a Diva (2)

a day in the life of a Diva (3)

a day in the life of a Diva (4)

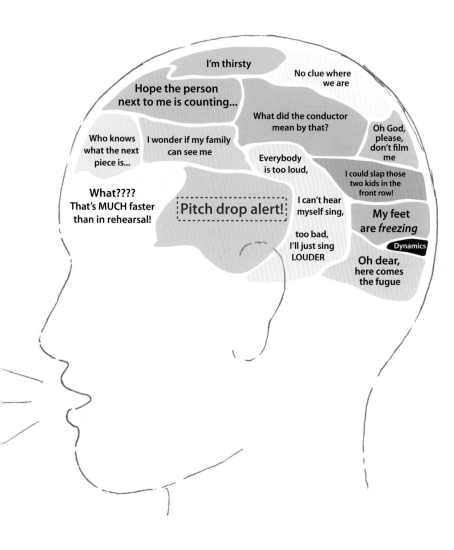

the choral singer's brain

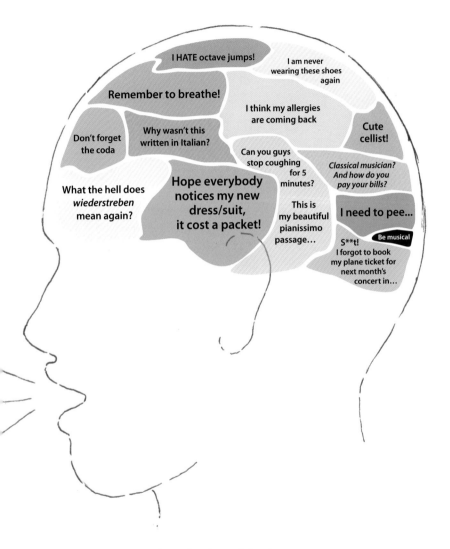

the solo singer's brain

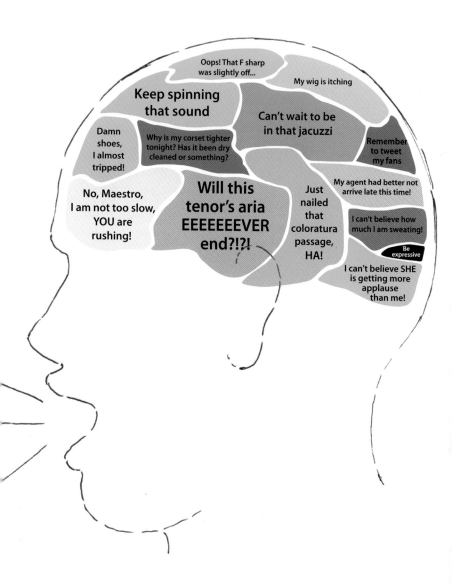

the opera singer's brain

OUR BELOVED AUDIENCE

the voice teacher: he / she who taught us everything!

those who bring us harmony

our many fellow musicians

the vocal coach & accompanist

the piano tuner

life-saving authors

the dresser

Before **After**

the hair & make-up artist

the sound engineer

...and everyone else, professional or amateur,
who shares our passion for SINGING!